EB-5 Visas & Real Estate Development

Rodrigo Azpúrua

DEDICATION

To my beloved wife, who has always supported each and
every one of my ideas (including this book).

To my Dad, who taught me how to think BIG.

To my sons Rodrigo Jose, Enrique Alejandro and Samuel
Andres. Their unconditional love enlightens me to move
forward no matter what.

To my Lord Jesus Christ, who strengthens me.

CONTENTS

HOW TO READ THIS BOOK

Since the reactivation of the EB-5 Visa Program in 2009, 308 Regional Centers have been created and approved by USCIS, but not more than 30 of them have been able to secure green cards for their investors.

Apart from the enormous and complicated legalities that are involved with the program, it's crucial to have the fundamentals for a successful real estate development in place prior to setting out to raise funds through overseas investors who are seeking a green card.

The initial chapters address these fundamentals. From chapter 7 on, you'll find an explanation of the program and practical insights to put into action when looking to engage in EB-5 Visas as an alternative way of financing deals.

INTRODUCTION

The 2008 Recession and EB-5 as Alternative Capital

In 1996, Alan Greenspan, then-Chairman of the Federal Reserve, described the frenzy and greed that stock investors feel at the top of a bull market as "*Irrational Exuberance*," coining the phrase in his speech to the American Enterprise Institute.

This irrational exuberance caused investors to overlook deteriorating economic fundamentals in the pursuit of ever higher returns. In doing so, the frenzy turned to panic and fear, which drove investors to sell at any cost, collapsing stock market prices and inevitably spreading the crash to the entire economy.

Irrational exuberance in pursuit of the pride of owning a home led many people to buy houses they couldn't afford. The aggressiveness of lenders reached an extreme in creating loans for *NINJAS*, people with *No Income and No*

Jobs. Many people didn't hesitate to buy a second, a third and many more houses, operating under the misconception that housing prices could only go *up*. In 2006, housing prices started to decline, and the bubble burst. Many homeowners, who had taken loans with little or no money down, found themselves owing the bank far more than the home's value. When many realized they would lose money by selling the house for less than the amount of their mortgage, the foreclosure rate escalated. Many banks and hedge funds panicked; they had bought mortgage-backed securities on the secondary market and now realized they were facing huge losses.

Following the burst came the credit crunch. By August 2007, banks feared lending to one another because they knew the only collateral available was the toxic loans they had created. This lack of circulating cash led to the $700 billion bailout, and bankruptcies or government nationalization of Bear Stearns, AIG, Fannie Mae, Freddie Mac, IndyMac Bank, and Washington Mutual.

By December 2008, employment was declining faster than in the 2001 recession.

Like any other recession, this one caused a decline in GDP growth, a slowdown in manufacturing orders, falling housing prices and sales, and a drop in business investment. Additionally, rising unemployment cut into retail sales, which created a downward spiral in manufacturing, increased layoffs and, of course, spurred the stock market decline.

In the aftermath, the corporations and small businesses that couldn't handle the crash had disappeared. Those able to reinvent their business and products, and tailor

2

their strategy to the new U.S. economy and it challenges, were ready to move toward growth and expansion. Certain metropolitan areas with the right type of industry were again building demand for real estate, be it housing and/or commercial space.

Real estate developers facing the lack of bank loans for construction sought alternative ways to finance development. Some of them began selling condos to overseas buyers, asking up to 80% of the sale price at preconstruction and using such funds to construct the building.

Other developers pursued foreign investors to bring their capital into the United States, in accordance with the USCIS EB-5 program (Employment Based Immigration). Their experience showed that to be successful, these entrepreneurs had to work toward a long-term vision and engage with a team of well qualified consultants, including immigration attorneys, corporate attorneys, SEC compliance officers, economists, accountants, marketing people, etc. They also needed extraordinary patience to deal with the Federal agencies' processing pace, which was often out of synch with the pace needed by the development itself.

For those who now choose this path, the following chapters are intended to help and guide them through the many challenges of the USCIS regulations and requirements, including job creation based on tenant occupancy.

1
VISION

As long as you're going to be thinking anyway, think big.

Donald Trump

In order to start a new land development project, it's crucial to Good entrepreneurs foresee "something out there," vague as it might appear from a distance, that others don't see.

A well-conceived vision consists of two major components: core ideology and envisioned future. The first defines what we stand for and why we exist. The second, the envisioned future, is what we aspire to become, to achieve, and to create; something that will require significant change and progress to attain.

Envisioned Future

In successful real estate development, the first step for the envisioned future is site selection. While many books have been written and this book devotes a chapter to this topic, it's worth noting that the first step in site selection begins in the mind and heart of the project leader, the developer.

Know how to identify and cultivate a project vision, one that must be aligned with your corporate and personal vision. But where do such visions originate? According to Burt Nanus, a vision is "a realistic, credible, attractive future for your organization. It is your articulation of a destination toward which your organization should aim, a future that is better, more successful, or more desirable for your organization than is the present."

Nanus contends that the right vision "is an idea so energizing that it in effect jump-starts the future by calling forth the skills, talents, and resources to make it happen."

After meetings and conversation with many developers, I've found all of them approach a land development and create their vision of it in one of the two following scenarios:

1.) A piece of land is identified or found; a market research study is performed to determine the best use, in light of the community's needs and the surrounding area. A full due diligence process then assures that the entitlements of the land exist, or can be achieved, for the product that suits the market need.

2.) The developer already has a product that he or she likes or knows how to manage -- be it retail, warehouses, offices or multifamily -- then "hunts" for a suitable tract of land. After researching available sites, the choice is narrowed, and market studies and finally due diligence follow.

I was part of an organization that had the vision to develop office buildings in high-end suburban markets in the State of Florida. I spent much time traveling throughout Florida doing market research, visiting sites, verifying demographic statistics, meeting with municipalities, local chambers of commerce and brokers, etc. We were successful in that process.

In 2010, I decided to start a new development and fund it with foreign private equity, following the guidelines of a federal program from the USCIS called EB-5. Such guidelines are very specific and require that the site be located in a Targeted Employment Area (TEA), a census tract with an unemployment rate equal or above 150 percent of the national average rate. While this requirement greatly constrained the search for a good property to develop, we finally identified one after thorough due diligence.

The best use that we identified for the parcel was development of an office building. I had been managing this same type of property, and it's where the majority of my experience and knowledge is based. This coincidence made me believe that everything happens for a reason, and there is already a planned purpose for everything that we do.

Core Values

The other element of your vision, the core ideology, defines the enduring character of an organization -- a consistent identity that transcends product or market life cycles, technological breakthroughs, management fads and individual leaders.

Core values are the essential and lasting tenets of an organization. As a concise set of timeless guiding principles, they have intrinsic value and importance to those inside the organization.

The execution of land development projects can bring many challenges throughout the process, from design, governmental approvals, to bidding and negotiating with general contractors or the subcontractors. At certain points, these may seem to be impossible to resolve. It's easy to get discouraged, but it is at these times that developers and project managers must refuse to give up.

This drive is only achievable by understanding the organization's set of values and following them with conviction. They will keep us focused on the envisioned future and not on the many problems to be overcome.

"Though outwardly we are wasting away, yet inwardly we are being renewed day by day." Saint Paul

As a sample or guide to create your own vision, the following are the values that I've used as the foundation for my organization.

Knowledge and Research: We gather, retrieve and evaluate a wider array of real estate market information that will provide accurate support for the investment decision process. We perceive market changes as opportunities for growth.

Discipline and Methodology: Executing our strategies is based on operations with disciplined, standardized, and consistent processes that are continuously reviewed and revised to assure the timely deliverance of our products, within budget and with the desired level of quality.

Customer Orientation: By connecting with our customers and understanding their needs and the different ways to use commercial real estate space, we can develop the right product for them.

Technology: To improve operational efficiency, we use state-of-the-art software.

Loyalty: We build long lasting relationships with all the valued parties that are involved with us in great endeavors such as these real estate projects.

Faith: Faith is the confidence that what we hope for will actually happen. It gives us assurance about things we cannot see. By faith, we understand that the entire universe was formed at God's command, that what we now see did not come from anything that can be seen.

I had attended many conferences and seminars, read books and listened to tapes, but the quest for a personal and organizational vision was never fulfilled through those means. "Personal vision," writes Doug Banister, "ultimately comes from one place: intimate communion with God."

Write down your vision and your core values. Use them as a foundation as you seek a site, so you can envision its future in the context of your organization's big picture. It's not enough to think about your vision and values; you must write them down to assure your envisioned future comes to pass.

2
PROJECT CONCEPUTUALIZATION

Disneyland is a work of love. We didn't go into Disneyland just with the idea of making money.

Walt Disney

When assessing which aspect of a land development project has the greatest ability to influence the cost, the answer without doubt is **conceptualization.** It sets the very quality of the product that will be delivered. Many developers have the impression that it is negotiating the bidding, or the construction itself, but the real element driving cost of a project is determining what we will deliver.

Quality

The product to be delivered is basically classified by property type, based on residential or commercial use. Commercial has four broad divisions: retail, office, warehouse and multifamily. The quality of the product to be delivered must be understood as the capacity to fulfill the end user's needs.

If the end user is a local restaurant, the product's quality will be driven by location to attract clients, good exposure, easy access and ample parking. The building itself must have a grease trap and fire-rated walls in the kitchen area. Defining the square footage to be allocated to meet a specific user's needs, be it a restaurant or a retail showroom in a shopping center, will impact the final cost of the development. These elements must be considered from the beginning.

Project Stakeholders

Many parties are involved in the property's financial destiny, and all of them have different perspectives. The owner looks for high occupancy and high rental rates, while the tenant seeks a cheap occupancy cost. The brokers want all business variables within the range of the market in order to make deals. The investors seek a higher return on their money, and the banks' underwriters look primarily at the risks to a feasible exit strategy.

So the developer envisioning the future has to work within the constraints that satisfy all these perspectives to assure the project's success. Still, there are more variables to consider. **I recommend a full Market analysis be completed prior to starting to work on the project concept.**

This process also takes leadership, a strong word and a difficult role to perform. The majority of development team members are outsourced professionals, and there is a non-hierarchical relationship among them. It is important to integrate them as a team and provide leadership, something that can be disputed by many team members if the project leader is not clear on his vision or his core values. One of the first and key challenges to face is if the developer's vision is in conflict with the vision of the architect, who is the team member with great influence on the design of the project. This is a very sensitive issue when brainstorming happens at the project concept stage.

I have personally worked with several "top-tier" architectural firms from all around the State of Florida, and all are smart and creative, up to date on new trends and always eager to design a building that will make everyone proud. But their design vision and perspective is not the only one to consider. In order to conceive a successful project, it's important that design not be allowed to override other factors -- the market is crucial, and the type of user is a key component.

Think about all the warehouse space that surrounds any airport; let's say Miami's International Airport. The majority of these warehouse tenants are freight forwarding companies or other types of corporations importing and exporting merchandise. Their requirements as tenants are completely different than for a tenant in the marine industry locating in a warehouse building in the Fort Lauderdale area. Both buildings may look similar, but rollover doors have different dimensions, bay heights are different, electric loads and meters are different. It's not the same warehouse building, and it's not the same product.

It's important that align the architect's vision with our own, but we also need to identify what our potential tenants envision as end users. The best way to understand this is through market analysis that includes interviews and conversations with property managers and/or real estate brokers who have been dealing for years with various tenant types in the area. This approach provides a real grasp of the current market.

Green Buildings

Social responsibility is our duty as individuals and in our organizations, to maintain a balance between the economy and the ecosystem. It's important to understand the requirements of the United States Green Building Council (USGBC) to develop a "Green Building". We don't live alone on this planet, and if we want the resources to last, we need to be conscious of and act on its needs. Using sustainable ("green") policies in our lives, in our offices and in our new land development projects is a good and feasible practice that I encourage everyone to follow.

Conclusion

Shape your vision with your team members' input and with the input of solid market research. Stay strong on what you believe, so the conception and design of your product has the best potential to fulfill the space user's needs for a high quality building.

3
MARKETING PLAN

If an ad campaign is built around a weak idea – or as is so often the case, no idea at all – I don't give a damn how good the execution is, it's going to fail.

Morris Hite,
Former Chairman, President & CEO, Tracy-Locke

It may seem too early to think about marketing in the project's concept stage, but the marketing plan is actually a key tool at this point. To take Hite's point a step further, early market analysis is a fundamental requirement for developing a product that will be used and accepted by the final consumer, the tenant.

This chapter addresses a group of questions that developers should be able to answer in no more than four pages. Answering them is a journey that you will enjoy and that will lead you to understand how much you know about your project and your product, how to adjust to market needs, and how to let the right people know that you are developing what they need.

Questions 1 thru 7 will help shape your product and provide some guidelines for performing market research and subsequent analysis.

Questions 8 thru 12 are intended to be completed by the marketing experts on the team. It is crucial to define these issues at the project's planning stage so cost and time frame can be accurately projected. These answers will also help identify needed design deliverables, such as renderings from the building's street view, bird's eye view, floor plans, etc.

Marketing Questionnaire

1. COMPANY NAME:
2. PROMOTIONAL STATEMENT:
3. PRODUCT DESCRIPTION:
   a. What do we sell?
   b. What are the benefits of our products?
   c. What is special about our product?
   d. Unique Selling Proposition (USP)
4. TARGET MARKET DEFINITION:
   a. Demographic Profile for Primary and Secondary Customers
   b. Where are they actually located?
   c. Who are our best customers and prospects?
5. MARKET ANALYSIS:
   a. Industry Background and Description
   b. Current Market Situation: How large is the overall market for this project?
   c. Market Segments:
      i. Who are our competitors?

        ii. What do our competitors do better than we do?

        iii. What is our competitive position?

        iv. What is our market share?

        v. Is our market shrinking, increasing or stable?

        vi. How do our prices compare with our competitors?

        vii. How do we establish our prices?

    d. Competitive Analysis (Strengths weaknesses, opportunities and threats):

        i. Our Business Strength

        ii. Our Business Weaknesses

        iii. What might keep us from achieving our goals?

        iv. Is the market changing in any way?

        v. What facts or new information do we need to figure out?

6. MARKETING/BUSINESS OBJECTIVES:

    a. Revenues/Sales

    b. Profits

    c. Market Share

7. SALES PLAN:

    a. Prospect identification

    b. Creating Awareness *(efforts toward building audience understanding, influencing opinion and motivating behavior)*

    c. Creating Conviction (The customer must be drawn to the conclusion that they must buy from us and us alone.)

    d. What are our sales practices?

8. **CREATIVE STRATEGY:** (How will we communicate our marketing message?) A decision must be made to self-perform or outsource these services.
    a. Unique Selling Proposition (USP)
    b. Copy/Tone Theme
    c. Visual/Image
    d. Incentive

9. **MEDIA COMMUNICATIONS STRATEGY/TACTICS:**
    a. Internet
    b. Print
    c. TV /Cable
    d. Direct Mail
    e. Radio
    f. Outdoor
    g. Miscellaneous

10. **OTHER MARKETING ACTIVITIES:**
    a. Trade Shows
    b. Event Marketing
    c. Public Relations
    d. Telemarketing
    e. Cause Related Marketing
    f. Personal Selling
    g. Collateral Material
    h. Promotions
    i. Ongoing Marketing Research

11. **BUDGET:** How much will your marketing effort cost? What percentage of sales?

12. SCHEDULE: Graphically depict a summary of your marketing activities by month.

Conclusion

Based on the questionnaire, it no doubt seems there is a lot of work ahead. That's true, but by thoroughly answering these questions, you'll gain greater confidence that your project will be well executed and attract quality tenants.

4
FINANCIAL FEASIBILITY

Did you ever think that making a speech on economics is a lot like pissing down your leg? It seems hot to you, but it never does to anyone else.

President Lyndon B. Johnson

Financial feasibility analysis is the very first step to take, even before trying to make an offer for the land. That's because such analysis answers the very crucial questions: "Should I go for this business idea? Will I finish this project with a profit or a loss?"

As unreasonable as it may sound, I've seen many developers of all types of properties, and many business owners in other industries, spending a dollar to create a product with 70 cents value, or even less. If you haven't experienced this, you're doing great, but ask any land developer who was doing business in late 2005 to 2008, in any city or town in the United States, about his experience. He'll likely tell you how construction prices were extremely high; everyone was paying high prices and after the deflation of the 2008 crisis, all property was worth 60%, 50% or even 30% of what it cost to build. Fortunes were lost.

But it doesn't take a .great recession to lose money on a land development project. Failure to do the proper due diligence may omit important facts on functional aspects of a project, for example, impact fees, or environmental issues such as wetlands. These items can have a tremendous impact on a project's financial feasibility. The same bad ending results when market feasibility analysis is inaccurate, leading to a situation where the proposed amount of space cannot be filled, or the rental rates necessary to obtain a profit are not being paid by tenants in the area.

Successful developers perform proper due diligence for every facet of the project. In this work we'll address two broad aspects: market feasibility and functional feasibility.

Market Feasibility

Market research and analysis is the process of gathering information with the purpose of identifying if there is a need for certain types of property. In other words, it determines if the current supply satisfies the demand or, if there is a shortage a profit can be made by adding certain types of property to the current inventory.

I always do deep market studies for all projects that I've developed or managed from beginning to end. It takes that fact-based assessment to find the market need, see the potential profit and understand its financial feasibility, so the envisioned project can match true market needs.

A market research study should have a structured, logical order. For me, it works well to break this into three parts.

Understand the Market

This part gathers all the information necessary to develop a broad and basic overview of the competitive environment. It provides the necessary foundation to provide more in-depth analysis of different business and real estate sectors. Data includes:

>Trade Area Analysis
>Demographics & Lifestyle Analysis
>Local & Regional Economic Analysis
>Business Owners Survey
>Consumer Survey
>Focus Groups
>Peer City Comparison

Analyze Opportunities by Sector

Go beyond providing information to analyze specific business and real estate development opportunities identified in Part I. The purpose here is to provide advanced data that can be used as part of a market analysis, or on an as-needed basis. Tools include methods for analyzing opportunities in:

>Retail & Service Businesses
>Restaurants
>Arts & Entertainment
>Housing
>Office Space
>Lodging
>Warehouses

Make Your Research Work

Develop conclusions and recommendations that are realistic in today's marketplace. The intent is to look "outside of the box" to identify realistic solutions that could impact your market. Tools include ways to apply market analysis data in:

> Niche Development
> Space Usage
> Image, Branding, Marketing
> Business Retention/Expansion
> Entrepreneurship
> Business Recruitment
> Benchmarking

While I was doing a presentation to raise funds for the Professional Center at Riviera Point, an office park in the City of Miramar Florida, I ran into a real estate attorney based in Broward County, Florida whose practice is dedicated exclusively to marketing of projects that qualify for the EB-5 program of the USCIS. In the middle of my presentation he looked at the market study charts and said to me, "These are great. They look very good, but no one knows what it means." At the time, I thought that was a lame statement, yet realized it could be true.

This chapter is intended to show you don't need to have years of statistical education to wrap your head around a well executed market study. A solid study will clarify if there is a need in the market for your project and if there is a profit to be made by providing this inventory. The right approach will help you create judgment criteria to understand the study data and draw a conclusion to support the decision to proceed or not move forward with the project and the investment..

Five broad items must be taken into consideration; this outline from the CCIM Institute explains:

1) Geographic area for which the data is presented.
    a. Formal: these are the established political boundaries such as the nation, state, county, cities, Metropolitan Statistical Areas, Consolidated Metropolitan Statistical Areas, Census Tract, Zip codes.
    b. Segmentation or Functional Regions: these are chosen and established by the analyst and are defined by considering the area from which the majority of business will come to support the site's use. The most common are the radius (around the site) and the driving distance (contemplates the traffic factors that influence how people will drive to the site).

2) Demographics:
    a. This means to "describe the people" and this data includes population statistics by age, race, sex, education, occupation, income, house value, etc.

3) Jobs (Employment):
    a. It's important to understand the causes and effects that create demand. Economists use employment as the primary predictor

of real estate demand because it starts a chain reaction. Job picture: First identify the basic industries and businesses that bring export-oriented income into a community. Measure their relative importance to the local economy, and identify any employment changes due to projected changes in these basic industries. Then forecast the impact and the resulting changes in the area's total employment. In this way, the demand for office and warehouse space (based also on the type of employment) can be determined. The impact of such employment change on total population projection will define the retail space demand.

b. Basic Employment: Jobs in industries with activities that produce more goods and services than can be consumed in the local area. The money basic employment brings into the local market drives the local economy.

c. Non-Basic Employment: Activities that produce goods for the local economy, production for internal consumption.

4) Vacancy Rates:

a. This is the number of square feet available for occupancy at a certain point in time, usually the present, and is expressed as a percentage of the total supply.

      b.   If vacancy increases: the supply is increasing or there is a loss of basic employment.

      c.   If vacancy decreases: An expansion in the market is occurring and the demand is increasing due to rapid growth in basic industries, with resulting impact on the non-basic sector.

5) Absorption:

      a.   This is the amount of inventory measured either by unit or square footage that becomes occupied during a specific time period, either a quarter or a year. Absorption is often expressed in market reports with the acronym YTD (year to date).

      b.   This data helps to determine the amount of new square footage or units that can be added every year.

      c.   Absorption is calculated by subtracting the total number of units occupied at the beginning of the year compared to the total number of units (or square feet) occupied at the end of the year.

Conclusion

If a market study is presented for your consideration for an investment or as the basis for a "go ahead" decision for your land development project, you must look at *all* the variables. I give special attention to these five variables to determine the need in the market. I encourage you to do the same.

And you'll see the value of doing so when we explain the Matter of Ho and the rigorous business planning that the USCIS requires from EB-5 Program petitioners.

All this effort will produce the assumptions that form the foundation of the business plan. Under the United States legal framework, such assumptions are considered and denominated **forward-looking statements.**

Forward-looking statements are based on current expectations and conclusions made from the research described in this chapter that involve a number of risks and uncertainties. Some of the assumptions are anticipation of market demand and that there will be no material adverse change in the anticipated approval from the local authorities.

Assumptions relating to the foregoing involve judgments relating to, among other things, future economic, competitive and market conditions and future business decisions, all of which are difficult or impossible to predict accurately and many of which are beyond your control as developer. But the assumptions are essential and are fundamentals of the business.

5
SITE SELECTION

I did not think I would understand the markets if I did not understand the inner thoughts of the people that formed those markets.

Luigi Salvaneschi

Site selection is a decision that has long-term implications for company owners and their employees and customers. Whether your tenants are searching for a site for a new business or relocation, the site you choose for your project should have the power to dramatically increase their profits by offering space at the right location with benefits to their main core trade.

But how can you tell if a site is a good location? First look to the defined objectives and target market for the project. In the big picture, the site must have the potential to provide future users with all they need to establish and/or grow their business. Then gather the detailed data to insure the site truly suits those potential tenants. The majority of corporations look for the following:

1. Real estate cost and availability, including rental rates, cost of the common area maintenance and vacancy rates.
2. Utilities cost as part of tenants' their day-to-day operations cost.
3. Transportation cost.
4. Labor cost, availability, union regulations, and workers' compensation rates.
5. Demographics including educational attainment level.
6. Tax structure and regulatory environment. Florida has no state income tax: *"It's not what you make, it's what you keep" W. Huizenga*
7. Economic development incentives.
8. Nearby universities (research) that will enhance the corporation's ability to recruit new talent, will help them in research and development of new products, processes and technologies, as well as best practices for leadership and management.
9. Quality Kindergarten up to 12th grade public and private education opportunities
10. Cultural amenities (arts and sports).
11. Cost of living and quality of life.
12. Airport proximity including airline flights to key markets.

A second level of more specific data is gathered by spotting the essential characteristics of the best location:

- Exposure: The property and the building must be seen by the majority of the public that transit in front of the site at any given time.
- Access: From both lanes; it can't be limited to

only one side of the street. It should have easy access from highways to broaden the trade zone.

- Traffic Count: Identify the volume of traffic, stay away from dead-ends and one-way streets. Also, look at the mix of traffic, and how people move from point to point in different ways that may influence the site's functionality.

Conclusion

Once all this data is gathered you need to create a valuation matrix, where each category is weighted in a predetermined scale to compare the different sites that you are considering.

This data comparison should be aligned with your project vision, your corporate values, your project financial objectives and your targeted clients' needs. Once all these variables are plugged in, you have the basis for sound decision-making. You are ready to make an offer on that site and go for it!

6
DUE DILIGENCE, THE KEY

Diligence is the mother of good luck.

Benjamin Franklin

One of the main objectives of performing due diligence prior to committing to the purchase is to ensure you get what you think you are paying for. It's the key path to financial feasibility, the gathering of all the information that will help us to determine if our business plan can be accomplished in a cost-effective manner.

The scope, intensity and focus of any due diligence investigation on a land tract or a parcel depend upon the objectives. By now, you should have already set these objectives, which may be based either on seeking to add value by changing the character or use of the property, usually with a short-term, intermediate or long-term exit strategy to dispose of it, or by developing and building on the property.

Next, focus on the main items/issues that MUST be investigated to gain a clear understanding of each before purchasing any type of property:

THE PROPERTY: Should be *exactly* the property which the purchaser believes he is acquiring. If land, this means the entire fee title interest, including all air rights and subterranean rights, and all development rights. Keep in mind that not all development rights are applicable to all parcels and may differ by location.

Prior to the start of a project, the development manager may be called upon by the owner/client and/or developer's strategic consultant to participate in reviewing sites under consideration.

PHYSICAL DATA

A. Area
    1. Major Features of Surrounding Properties or Region
    2. Demographics/Statistics

B. Physical Features
    (Sources: FEMA Maps, Physical Site Walk-Through, etc.)
    1. Topography
    2. Drainage:
        a. Natural
        b. Man-made
    3. Existing Structures:
        a. Historical
        b. Demolition
        c. Adaptive reuse
    4. Subsoil Conditions (Sources: existing geotechnical and environmental reports:
        a. Geotechnical

      b.   Environmental
5. Trees (note quality and size/caliper)
6. Plantings and Ground Cover
7. Low Areas, Ground Water/Wetlands
8. Obstructions
9. Overhead Utilities (i.e., do they need to be buried and can they be buried?)
      a.   Existing
      b.   Future
10. Waste Disposal Systems (sewer, septic, other) 11. Air Pollution Control

C. Design/Construction Considerations
  1. Grading
      a.   Import/Export
      b.   Cut/fill
  2. Site Preparation
  3. Material Storage
      a.   Lay down
      b.   Assembly
      c.   Refuse/Rubbish
  4. Utility Protection or Relocation
  5. Planting Protection
  6. Public Protection (e.g., barricades, site enclosure fencing, roving security guard)
      a.   Site enclosure fencing
      b.   Pedestrian barricades
      c.   Temporary Access Locations
  7. Protection of Adjacent Facilities
      a.   Retaining Walls
      b.   Foundations
      c.   Excavations
      d.   Tiebacks
  8. Expansion or Phasing Considerations
      a.   Short Term (1 -3 years)
      b.   Long Term (3 - 5 years)

9. Orientation Possibilities
   a. Visibility/Recognition from public streets or highways
   b. Views - preferred or blocked
   c. Sun/weather considerations
10. Parking
    a. Surface
    b. Structured
    c. Security concerns
    d. Distance to facilities
    e. Maintenance/operations
11. Demolition
    a. Responsibility
    b. Inspection/Testing after completion

12. Existing Structures
    a. Demolition
    b. Re-use
    c. Protection during construction

D. Utilities
   [Note: the project manager should obtain specific information on the utility companies delivering the following services. At a minimum, collect the following for each provider: :
   -Name of Supplier/Company with address and phone numbers
   -Proximity of service to subject site
   -Existing capacity
   -Future increases to capacity and timing
   -Is this supplier the original generator/receiver, or are they dependent upon another utility company?

Do not overlook the last item noted above, since continued changes in utility suppliers and generators may mean that the local firm you're dealing with only purchases the supply. Other regional or statewide firms/networks may be the provider.

Providers may include:
1. Water
2. Sanitary Sewer
3. Storm Sewer
4. Electricity
5. Natural Gas
6. Telephone
7. Cable Television
8. Other

LEGAL

Project Managers should cite all ordinances, restrictions, covenants, laws, etc. by number and reference them to the appropriate source for all subject matter within this section. Whenever possible a photocopy of supporting information or data should be attached as exhibits to the report.

A. Zoning (Source: Department of Planning and Zoning)
1. Present
2. Required
3. Zoning Map and Ordinance

B. Covenants, Restrictions, Right-of-Way, Easements (Sources: title policy, recorder of deeds; surveys)
1. Roads
2. Utility
3. Air
   a. Ownership of the "air rights" to build above the land

4. Subsurface:
    a. Ownership of the "mineral rights" to collect beneath surface.
5. Other

C. Code Requirements in Effect
    1. Local
    2. County
    3. State
    4. Public Health
    5. Fire
    6. Other

D. Permits and Fees
    1. Building Permits (Source: Municipal or County Permit Dept.)
    2. Utility Tap-in Fees
    3. Impact Fees (County)
    4. Other

E. Taxes
    1. Current
    2. Upon Full Build-Out
    3. During Construction
        a. Exemptions for sale taxes on materials
        b. Value added

Conclusion

It is critically important to conduct an effective due diligence investigation in a commercial or industrial real estate transaction to discover all material facts and conditions affecting the Property and the transaction.

Unlike owner-occupied residential real estate, which can

nearly always be occupied as the purchaser's home, commercial and industrial real estate acquired for business use or for investment is impacted by numerous factors that may limit its use and value.

The existence of these factors and their impact on a purchaser's ability to use the property as intended can only be discovered through diligent and focused investigation and attention to details.

7

EB-5: DEFINITION OF THE IMMIGRANT INVESTOR PROGRAM

America was indebted to immigration for her settlement and prosperity. That part of America which had encouraged them most had advanced most rapidly in population, agriculture and the arts.
James Madison

This chapter is not intended to be a legal text or to supersede legal counsel and advice from qualified consultants/attorneys. Its intent is to explain in layman's terms what the program is about. To find accurate legal definitions, refer to the USCIS website where you can find copies of documents including section 203(b) (5) of the Immigration and Nationality Act (INA), 8 U.S.C. §1153(b) (5).

The Immigrant Investor Program, also known as the EB-5 program of the USCIS, states that every qualifying foreign national who invests one million U.S. Dollars (US $1,000,000) in a company or project that creates ten (10) permanent jobs in the next several months can obtain conditional residency status. This conditional green card grants the applicant the same rights as a permanent resident, except that it is limited in time to two years. Ninety days prior to the expiration deadline, the applicant must apply again to the USCIS to convert the conditional green card into a permanent green card by proving the job creation requirement has been met.

USCIS works based on quotas, either numerical and/or by country. Currently, ten thousand (10,000) EB-5 immigrant visas are allocated annually to alien investors and the spouse and qualifying children of the investor. EB-5 status is available on a first-come, first-served basis. If more visas are sought than are available, it will result in a delay in the availability of EB-5 lawful permanent resident status.

Like everything else relating to governmental results anywhere in the world, there is no reliable means to predict if such a delay will occur -- or if it occurs, how long an investor or the investor's spouse and qualifying children will wait before visa status becomes available. Also, the availability of current EB-5 immigrant visas may end; the number of available EB-5 immigrant visas may change, and the time it takes to acquire EB-5 status may increase significantly.

The current law provides the applicability of a country quota if the 10,000 visa cap is reached on an annual fiscal basis. If the cap were reached, under current legislation the 7% per country quota limitations would become operative and therefore put a maximum on EB-5 visas issued for investors from specific nations during such calendar year. Since it is estimated that for fiscal year 2012 up to 80% of the EB-5 visas were issued to Chinese nationals, this limitation could result in a serious and adverse effect of marketing the EB-5 Program in China.

Legislation has previously been proposed to eliminate the per-country quota and we are actively working and supporting the civil organization IIUSA to support passage of such legislation.

If the investment is made through a Regional Center and in a Target Employment Area (TEA), the investment to qualify can be five hundred thousand U.S. Dollars (US$500,000) rather than $1,000,000.

At the USCIS website, you'll find the following information:

USCIS administers the Immigrant Investor Program, also known as "EB-5," created by Congress in 1990 to stimulate the U.S. economy through job creation and capital investment by foreign investors. Under a pilot immigration program first enacted in 1992 and regularly reauthorized since, certain EB-5 visas also are set aside for investors in Regional Centers designated by USCIS based on proposals for promoting economic growth.

All EB-5 investors must invest in a **new commercial enterprise**, which is a commercial enterprise established after Nov. 29, 1990, or established on or before Nov. 29, 1990, that is: Purchased and the existing business is restructured or reorganized in such a way that a new commercial enterprise results, or expanded through the investment so that a 40-percent increase in the net worth or number of employees occurs.

Commercial enterprise means any for-profit activity formed for the ongoing conduct of lawful business including, but not limited to: A sole proprietorship, partnership (whether limited or general), holding company, joint venture, corporation, business trust or other entity, which may be publicly or privately owned.

This definition includes a commercial enterprise consisting of a holding company and its wholly owned subsidiaries, provided that each such subsidiary is engaged in a for-profit activity formed for the ongoing conduct of a lawful business.

Note: This definition does not include noncommercial activity such as owning and operating a personal residence.

Capital Investment Requirements

Capital means cash, equipment, inventory, other tangible property, cash equivalents and indebtedness secured by assets owned by the alien entrepreneur, provided that the alien entrepreneur is personally and primarily liable and that the assets of the new commercial enterprise upon which the petition is based are not used to secure any of the indebtedness. All capital shall be valued at fair-market value in United States Dollars.

Assets acquired, directly or indirectly, by unlawful means (such as criminal activities) shall not be considered capital for the purposes of section 203(b)(5) of the Act. Note: Investment capital cannot be borrowed.

When traveling around the world, working hard to raise capital for a project, you'll find all kinds of people and capital sources. **Only one kind can be accepted – the one that comes from lawful means**. Fortunately, the law reinforces that concept.

Evidence must support the legal acquisition of capital. Funds earned or obtained in the United States while the investor had unlawful immigration status are not deemed to be lawfully acquired. If funds are not lawfully acquired, they may not be deemed "at risk."

As mentioned above, the required minimum investments are:

General: The minimum qualifying investment in the United States is $1 million.

Targeted Employment Area (High Unemployment or Rural Area): The minimum qualifying investment either within a high-unemployment area or rural area in the United States is $500,000.

A **targeted employment** area is an area that, at the time of investment, is a rural area or an area experiencing unemployment of at least 150 percent of the national average rate.

A **rural area** is any area outside a metropolitan statistical area (as designated by the Office of Management and Budget) or outside the boundary of any city or town having a population of 20,000 or more according to the decennial census.

.

8

WHO IS EXCLUDED BY LAW FROM
APPLYING FOR AN EB-5 VISA

"I don't want anyone who doesn't want me."
— Oprah Winfrey

The ultimate purpose of the EB-5 program is attract capital and a strong and qualified entrepreneurial population. Around the world, though, not everyone who has such capital to invest can be considered or qualified by immigration laws to apply for lawful permanent residence. The individual investor must overcome the statutory presumption of inadmissibility.

Applicants for EB-5 visas must demonstrate, affirmatively, that they are admissible to the United States. There are many grounds of inadmissibility that the government may cite as a basis to deny admission for lawful permanent residence. Various statutes, including for example Sections 212, 237 & 241 of the INA Act, the Antiterrorism & Effective Death Penalty Act of 1996 (AEDPA) and the Illegal Immigration Reform &

Immigrant Responsibility Act of 1996 (IIRAIRA) set forth grounds of inadmissibility, which may prevent an otherwise eligible applicant from receiving an immigrant visa, entering the United States or adjusting to lawful permanent residence.

According to the U.S. Immigration and Nationality Act, examples of aliens precluded from entering the United States include:

(a) persons who are determined to have a communicable disease of public health significance;

(b) persons who are found to have, or have had, a physical or mental disorder and behavior associated with the disorder which poses or may pose, a threat to the property, safety, or welfare of the alien or of others, or have had a physical or mental disorder and a history of behavior associated with the disorder, which behavior has posed a threat to the property, safety, or welfare of the immigrant alien or others, and which behavior is likely to recur or to lead to other harmful behavior.

(c) persons who have been convicted of a crime involving moral turpitude (other than a purely political offense), or persons who admit having committed the essential elements of such a crime.

(d) persons who have been convicted of any law or regulation relating to a controlled substance, admitted to having committed or admits committing acts which constitute the essential elements of same;

(e) persons who are convicted of multiple crimes (other than purely political offenses) regardless of whether the conviction was in a single trial or whether the offenses arose from a single scheme of misconduct and regardless of whether such offenses involved moral turpitude;

(f)   persons who are known, or for whom there is reason to believe, are, or have been, traffickers in controlled substances;

(g)   persons engaged in prostitution or commercialized vice;

(h)   persons who have committed in the United States certain serious criminal offenses, regardless of whether such offense was not prosecuted as a result of diplomatic immunity;

(i)   persons excludable on grounds related to national security, related grounds, or terrorist activities;

(j)   persons determined to be excludable by the secretary of state of the United States on grounds related to foreign policy;

(k)   persons who are or have been a member of a totalitarian party, or persons who have participated in Nazi persecutions or genocide;

(l)   persons who are likely to become a public charge at any time after entry;

(m)   persons who were previously deported or excluded and deported from the United States;

(n)   persons who by fraud or willfully misrepresenting a material fact, seek to procure (or have procured) a visa, other documentation or entry into the United States or other benefit under the Immigration Act;

(o)   persons who have at any time assisted or aided any other alien to enter or try to enter the United States in violation of law;

(p)   certain aliens who have departed the United States to avoid or evade U.S. Military service or training;

(q)   persons who are practicing polygamists;

(r)   persons who were unlawfully present in the United States for continuous or cumulative periods in excess of 180 days.

Options

Waivers are available for certain of the many grounds of inadmissibility, but the grant of a waiver is at the discretion of the government.

9
INDIVIDUALS INCLUDED IN THE APPLICATION FOR AN EB-5 VISA

Family is the most important thing in the world.
Princess Diana

We promote our EB-5 projects all around the world. With different airports, cultures, languages and food, all kinds of misunderstandings, good relations and real friendships come out of it. In South America, each time we finish a seminar presentation and I ask for questions, always, *always* a woman raises her hand and asks, "Does that green card include the wife and kids?" Fortunately. the answer is, "Yes, of course," with certain exceptions and conditions.

The Spouses of the investor may accompany or follow to join an investor who has been granted conditional lawful permanent residence. Under the understanding that the investor and the spouse, deemed a derivative beneficiary, were married at the time of the investor's first admission to the United States as a conditional lawful permanent resident or following adjustment of status to lawful permanent residence. USCIS will not recognize common law marriages for the purpose of permitting a spouse to be a qualifying derivative beneficiary. If the relationship is one of common law, the "spouse" of the investor may not acquire lawful permanent resident status on account of the relationship.

Expect the unexpected when it comes to relationships. In our Miramar, Florida project, a young investor's father was providing the EB-5 funding, and it took a while to submit the application. The young man's girlfriend wanted to get married, but he did not, so she wouldn't allow him to apply without her. The decision took time, until he finally maneuvered himself out of it and applied without getting married. They were married six months later in the U.S. There is no escaping destiny.

Children or step-children of the investor may accompany or follow to join an investor who has been granted conditional lawful permanent residence provided that the investor can establish parentage or step-parentage at the time of the investor's first admission to the United States as a conditional lawful permanent resident or adjustment of status to lawful permanent residence.

A Latin mother may see her 35-year-old son as her "child," but the law sees things differently. The legal definition is that a "child" is someone under the age of 21 years who is unmarried.

If a child becomes age 21 or marries before being admitted to the U.S. as a lawful permanent resident or adjusting to lawful permanent resident status, the former child, now deemed a son or daughter, may not be eligible to accompany or follow to join the investor. But there is an option -- the Child Status Protection Act -- that may assist a son or daughter to qualify as a child by reducing the deemed age of the son or daughter to less than 21 years.

This is a complicated formula that needs to be discussed with the immigration attorney prior to filing the application.

10
THE EB-5 VISA PROCESS

Mothers all want their sons to grow up to be president, but they don't want them to become politicians in the process.
John F. Kennedy

Step One: Vetting Funds and Doing the Investment

Investors seeking lawful permanent residence should establish proof and bring evidence to support the legal acquisition of capital. Funds earned or obtained in the United States while the investor was in unlawful immigration status are not deemed to be lawfully acquired. If funds are not lawfully acquired, they may not be deemed "at risk" and should not be accepted by the developer as capital investment.

To make the investment, the investor signs the contract, usually a subscription agreement of a share into a corporate entity, and wire transfers the money. Prior to the time the application is submitted to the USCIS, the petitioner must have invested the minimum required capital. USCIS expects these funds to be "at risk," connoting an irrevocable commitment to the enterprise.

The funds must be used by the enterprise exclusively to create employment. The petition must be supported by evidence of the investment already made.

Step Two: I-526 Petition Process

For investors seeking lawful permanent residency, the second step is filing an I-526 immigration Petition for Entrepreneur. This needs to happen after the Investor complies with the many requirements of the USCIS EB-5 program.

In addition to bringing evidence of the lawful means of their capital and the capital itself, investors must also comply with the following requirements:

Bring evidence that shows that the enterprise is new and is authorized to transact business in the territory of the Regional Center under the applicable terms and conditions of the EB-5 Program.

The investor is expected to participate in the management of the new enterprise by assisting in the formulation of the enterprise's business policy, by participating in one or more of the activities permitted by law in the state where the investment is being made, and as otherwise set forth in the Operating Agreement. In Florida, for example, investors in an EB-5 enterprise must have all the rights and duties usually accorded to members applicable under the Florida Limited Liability Company Act. The rights of the Investing Members under the Operating Agreement are consistent with rights normally granted to non-managers under the Florida Limited Liability Company Act.

Support the petition with evidence that the required minimum sum has been invested. If the amount is lower

than the minimum set by the law, the application will be
denied.

Show the potential to create the jobs. There must be
evidence that, as of the end of the two-year period of each
EB-5 investor's conditional residence (which is deemed
and projected by USCIS to be 2.5 years after adjudication
of the I-526 Petition), 10 full-time jobs will be created on
account of each EB-5 investment.

The I-526 Immigrant Petition for Entrepreneur will be
approved only if USCIS is satisfied that the foregoing
criteria have been met. The determination of whether
these criteria have been established is within the discretion
of USCIS. It is also within the power, if not the
discretionary authority, of USCIS to seek information
about other aspects of the investment and the relationship
of the investor to the enterprise. USCIS frequently
reinterprets the meaning of qualifying criteria. There can
be no certainty that compliance with the foregoing criteria,
supported by appropriate documentation, will lead to the
I-526 Petition Approval.

In the event that USCIS denies the I-526 Petition, the
investor may not proceed with the next step in the
immigration process, consular processing or adjustment of
status. Instead, the investor must decide whether to appeal
the I-526 Petition Denial at his or her own cost and
expense or abandon the prospect of investing in the
company and obtaining lawful permanent resident status
hereby.

Many EB-5 real estate development projects allow the
investor to place the money into an escrow account and
wait for positive response from USCIS regarding approval
of the I-526 petition to have access to the capital. And in

case of denial at this level of the process, the funds are returned.

Step Three: Consular Processing or Adjustment of Status – The Green Card

It is important to understand what it means to have an I-526 application approved. Many of my clients became confused about their rights once they receive this approval. I-526 Petition Approval means that the alien and the alien's spouse and children under the age of 21 years may apply for admission as conditional lawful permanent residents ("**CLPR**"). I-526 Petition Approval does not mean that the investor has been granted admission to the United States as a lawful permanent resident. Approval means that the investment documented by the I-526 Petition has qualified the investor as an alien entrepreneur.

Application for admission is a separate and subsequent process that concerns issues common to all aliens who wish to live in the United States permanently. Admission as a CLPR may be sought using one of two methods: **consular processing** or **adjustment of status**, as explained in the following information:

Consular Processing

Consular processing is designed for aliens who are living outside of the United States, who prefer to process at a consulate for strategic reasons or as a matter of convenience, or are ineligible to adjust status. Typically, the consular post, which is chosen at the time the I-526 Petition is filed, is in the country of last residence, *i.e.*, the last principal actual dwelling place. In very limited instances, usually involving a recognized hardship, a different consular post may be used to process for lawful permanent residence.

Before issuing an immigrant visa, the consular post must determine if each alien is admissible to the United States. I-526 Petition Approval does not by itself establish admissibility. An alien is admissible who proves that no grounds of inadmissibility exist and the alien has proper travel documents.

If the consular post finds that the investor is admissible, it will issue an immigrant visa to the investor. The consular post will also determine if the spouse and the qualifying children of the investor are admissible. A determination of admissibility must be made as to each visa applicant. There is no guarantee that all members of the investor's family will be granted an immigrant visa. If the investor is denied an immigrant visa, applications by the spouse and children of the investor for such a visa will be denied.

Consular processing begins when USCIS transmits the I-526 Petition Approval to the National Visa Center ("**NVC**"). At appropriate intervals, the NVC issues instructions and appointment packages and requests required documents and information. In time, the alien will be instructed to obtain fingerprints and a physical examination and to report to a consular interview. Immigrant visas usually are issued shortly after the interview unless the consul detects problems in the visa application, the underlying I-526 Petition or during the interview process. Visa applicants should allow about twelve months to complete consular processing, although times for processing vary greatly among consular posts.

Consul's decisions are discretionary. USCIS and DOS report recent efforts to communicate more efficiently regarding their respective roles in determining the eligibility of EB-5 investors for immigrant visas. There cannot be any assurance that improved communications will occur generally or with respect to a particular investor or the investor's spouse or minor children. Neither may it be assured that improved communications will result in the issuance of a visa. Other factors that a consul may, with unreviewable discretion, elect to consider could result in the denial of a visa.

Visa applicants should not change any living, employment, schooling or other lifestyle arrangements in their country of residence before they are issued an immigrant visa based upon an I-526 Petition Approval.

Adjustment of Status

The Adjustment of Status ("**AOS**") procedure is designed to permit aliens who have been admitted to the United States as non-immigrants or who have been paroled into the country to apply for admission as permanent residents without leaving the country. These non-immigrants must establish that they are admissible permanently, meeting the same standards as aliens who use consular processing to obtain a permanent resident visa.

Aliens seeking AOS must also comply with requirements particular to the AOS process. Aliens who do not meet these additional requirements will be required to use consular processing to obtain an immigrant visa, which will necessitate a departure from the United States. Aliens admitted in certain non-immigrant statuses may encounter more difficulties (and may not be successful) adjusting status than aliens admitted in other non-immigrant statuses. Investors should consult with immigration counsel regarding these issues before the I-526 Petition is filed.

During AOS processing, the applicant will be required to submit a medical examination and will receive instructions from USCIS regarding biometric data collection and an interview. USCIS uses profiling information to determine who will be interviewed and it also interviews some AOS applicants to maintain the integrity of its screening process. There is no formal process to request the waiver of an interview. If the investor is interviewed, the spouse and children of the investor will be required to attend the interview.

Travel During Adjustment of Status Processing

An alien investor who leaves the United States without advance permission while an AOS application is pending is deemed to have abandoned that application unless the applicant has been admitted in and continues to hold valid H or L non-immigrant status pending adjudication of the AOS application.

Advance permission to depart the U.S. is issued routinely if the alien articulates a *bona fide* need to travel. It is not necessary to demonstrate an emergent need to travel; any purpose not contrary to law is usually deemed sufficient. Advance permission, known as Advance Parole, is usually granted for multiple entries during the time required to complete the AOS process, but not longer than one year. It may be necessary to re-apply for Advance Parole if the AOS process is not complete within a year.

Advance Parole is not available to aliens who are outside the U.S. It is important for AOS applicants who wish the right to travel to make application for Advance Parole while they are in the U.S. They must remain in the U.S. until Advance Parole is granted to avoid abandonment of the AOS application. Advance Parole applications may take about 60-90 days to be granted. Processing times may be longer if an applicant is subjected to extended background checking. In demonstrated emergent circumstances, an AOS applicant may receive expedited Advance Parole.

Alien investors admitted to the United States in any non-immigrant status who have obtained Advance Parole during the AOS process should consult with immigration counsel before traveling. Re-admission to the U.S. using the Advance Parole document may jeopardize the non-immigrant status of the alien's family members who did not travel. The consequences, if any, of this situation should be examined prior to travel.

Employment During The Adjustment of Status Processing

Applicants for AOS who wish to work in the United States must obtain employment authorization unless they have been admitted to the U.S. in a non-immigrant status that confers employment authorization that does not end before AOS is granted. Self-employment requires employment authorization.

Employment authorization applications currently take 60-90 days to be adjudicated. Processing times may be longer if an applicant is subjected to extended background checking. Employment authorization is usually granted during the time required to complete the AOS process, but not longer than one year. It may be necessary to re-apply for employment authorization if the AOS process is not complete within a year. To avoid a lapse in employment authorization re-applications should be made sufficiently in advance of the expiry of existing authorization. Employment without authorization at any time in the U.S. is a violation of immigration status and may jeopardize the right to adjust status.

AOS applicants should not make any permanent connections to the United States or change any permanent living, employment, schooling or other lifestyle arrangements in their country of residence before they are issued AOS based upon an I-526 Petition Approval.

Step Four: Removal of Conditions, convert the conditional green card into a permanent status.

This is the final step and here is where the burden on the developer to meet the Job Creation requirement starts. Within two years, the project must have started, moved and created the jobs.

Once that is accomplished, and with the evidence that those jobs were created, the Investor, with counsel, needs to proceed to the removal of conditions that is sought by filing an I-829 Petition in the 90-day period immediately before the second anniversary of the grant of CLPR status. In support of the petition, the alien investor must demonstrate full investment in the enterprise and compliance with the requirement that 10 full-time jobs have been created as a result of the investment. The investor must also demonstrate maintenance of the investment continuously since becoming a CLPR.

USCIS currently has jurisdiction to decide a petition to remove conditions. It is authorized to approve a petition, seek additional written information before deciding the petition, refer the petition to a local office where information will be elicited in an interview, or it may deny the petition.

During the pendency of the petition, aliens admitted in CLPR Status remain in valid status even if the petition is not decided before the expiry of the two year period of admission. CLPR is extended in one year increments or until the petition to remove conditions is adjudicated.

Many of the foreign investors may be brave enough to do the investment, but not patient enough to endure the process. It's very important to report to them, keep them informed and support them thru the whole process.

11
JOB CREATION
REQUIREMENTS

With patient and firm determination, I am going to press on for jobs.
I'm going to press on for equality. I'm going to press on for the sake
of our children. I'm going to press on for the sake of all those families
who are struggling right now. I don't have time to feel sorry for myself.
I don't have time to complain. I am going to press on.

Barack Obama

It is important to take special note of the USCIS's strict job creation requirements, which are key to your EB-5 investors' ability to qualify for permanent residency. The USCIS details these requirements and definitions as:

Create or preserve at least 10 full-time jobs for qualifying U.S. workers within two years (or under certain circumstances, within a reasonable time after the two-year period) of the immigrant investor's admission to the United States as a Conditional Permanent Resident (1).

Create or preserve either direct or indirect jobs:

Direct jobs are actual identifiable jobs for qualified employees located within the commercial enterprise into which the EB-5 investor has directly invested his or her capital. **Indirect jobs** are those jobs shown to have been created collaterally or as a result of capital invested in a commercial enterprise affiliated with a regional center by an EB-5 investor. A foreign investor may only use the indirect job calculation if affiliated with a regional center.

Note: Investors may only be credited with preserving jobs in a troubled business.

A **troubled business** is an enterprise that has been in existence for at least two years and has incurred a net loss during the 12- or 24-month period prior to the priority date on the immigrant investor's Form I-526. The loss for this period must be at least 20 percent of the troubled business' net worth prior to the loss. For purposes of determining whether the troubled business has been in existence for two years, successors in interest to the troubled business will be deemed to have been in existence for the same period of time as the business they succeeded.

A **qualified employee** is a U.S. citizen, permanent resident or other immigrant authorized to work in the United States. The individual may be a conditional resident, a refugee, or a person residing in the United States under suspension of deportation. This definition does not include the immigrant investor; his or her spouse, sons, or daughters; or any foreign national in any nonimmigrant status (such as an H-1B visa holder) or who is not authorized to work in the United States.

Full-time employment means employment of a qualifying employee by the new commercial enterprise in a position that requires a minimum of 35 working hours per week. In the case of the Immigrant Investor Pilot Program, "full-time employment" also means employment of a qualifying employee in a position that has been created indirectly from investments associated with the Pilot Program (2).

A **job-sharing arrangement** whereby two or more qualifying employees share a full-time position will count as full-time employment provided the hourly requirement per week is met. This definition does not include combinations of part-time positions or full-time equivalents even if, when combined, the positions meet the hourly requirement per week. The position must be permanent, full-time and constant. The two qualified employees sharing the job must be permanent and share the associated benefits normally related to any permanent, full-time position, including payment of both workman's compensation and unemployment premiums for the position by the employer

---

[1] Immigration and Nationality Act (INA) § 203(b)(5); 8 U.S.C. § 1153(b)(5).

[2] Immigration Act of 1990, Pub. L. No. 101-649 (Nov. 29, 1990).

12
ECONOMETRIC
METHODOLOGIES

"Economic statistics are like a bikini,
what they reveal is important, what they conceal is vital"
Attributed to **Professor Sir Frank Holmes**, Victoria
University, Wellington, New Zealand, 1967

To understand the Econometric model and its impact, we can look to several sources as below:

To encourage use of the EB-5 visa category, Congress established the Immigrant Investor Pilot Program in 1993 and set aside 3,000 of the allocated 10,000 visas for investors who invest within designated "regional centers." This program eventually became referred to as the "Regional Center Pilot."

Under the pilot, foreign investors can pool their investments into Regional Centers, which make large investments that create jobs. Regional Center investors are permitted to demonstrate through "reasonable methodologies" that their investment resulted in the creation of ten or more direct or indirect jobs.

More specifically, investors within EB-5 Regional Centers are permitted to use statistical formulas and models to demonstrate a correlation between their investment of capital into a specific business and indirect jobs created in other businesses within the greater community. In Regional Center cases, these indirectly generated jobs may be used to satisfy the job creation requirement.

The **IMPLAN** model has long been accepted by the USCIS (and many other governmental agencies) as a valid economic methodology that satisfies the requirements of 8 CFR § 204.6(j)(4), 8 CFR § 204.6(m)(3)(iv) and 8 CFR § 204.6(m)(3)(v).

The IMPLAN system is a menu-driven microcomputer program that performs complex calculations in the methods and assumptions used to generate social accounts and Input/Output multipliers. The software performs the necessary calculations using the study area data to create the models. The system allows users to make in-depth examinations of regional, state, multi-county, county or sub-county economies.

The IMPLAN data and accounts closely follow the accounting conventions used in the "Input/Output Study of the U.S. Economy" by the Bureau of Economic Analysis and the rectangular format recommended by the United Nations.

Comprehensive and detailed data coverage of the entire U.S. by county and the ability to incorporate user supplied data at each stage of the model building process provides a high degree of flexibility both in terms of geographic coverage and model formulation.

IMPLAN is based on the concept of a production function, which determines the quantities of inputs that are required to produce a unit of output. The basic data are collected by the Commerce Department from a variety of sources, such as the Annual Survey of Manufacturers and various annual surveys of the service sector. The data are benchmarked to the Economic Census figures once every five years and then updated annually. These figures comprise a national input/output model.

All of this data is contained within the IMPLAN software developed by the Minnesota IMPLAN Group, Inc. The "processes and calculations" are thus embedded within the programming of the software which renders an "output" based on any "input" in the way a calculator contains mathematical rules for generating output based on data input. **To fully understand the complexity of the IMPLAN software and the mathematical models utilized to generate output data requires a deep knowledge of applied economic theory.**

The following material, taken from the IMPLAN manual, describes the input/output process in more detail.

> *Input/output analysis is a means of examining relationships within an economy, between businesses and between businesses and final consumers. It captures all of the monetary market transactions for consumption in a given time period. The resulting mathematical formulae allow for examination of the effects of a change in one or several economic activities on an entire economy.*
>
> *A descriptive model includes information about local economic interactions known as regional economic accounts. These describe a local economy in terms of the flow of dollars from purchasers to producers within the region. The initial IMPLAN data details all purchases, including*

imported goods and services. When regional economic accounts are created, imports to the region are removed from the initial data, allowing examination of local inter-industry transactions and final purchases.

The regional economic accounts are used to construct local level multipliers. Multipliers describe the response of the economy to a stimulus (a change in demand or production). The multipliers represent the Predictive Model.

Purchases for final use (final demand) drive an input/output model. Industries producing goods and services for consumption purchase goods and services from other producers. These other producers, in turn, purchase goods and services. These indirect purchases (or indirect effects) continue until leakages from the region (imports, wages, profits, etc.) stop the cycle.

The indirect effects and the effects of increased household spending (induced effects) can be mathematically derived as sets of multipliers.

The derivation is called the Leontief inverse. The resulting sets of multipliers describe the change of output for each industry caused by a one dollar change in final demand for any given industry.

The input/output analysis framework is similar to a financial accounting framework that tracks purchases of and expenditures on goods and services in dollars. Input/output accounting traces the flow of dollars between businesses and between businesses and final consumers.

Final Consumption (or final demand) drives input/output models. Industries respond to meet demand directly or indirectly, by supplying goods and services to industries responding directly. Each industry that produces goods and services generates demands for other goods and services, and so on. Multipliers describe these iterations.

The IMPLAN model needs to be used for USCIS purposes in a way that generates output data in the form of job creation and economic impact numbers. The IMPLAN software derives monetary predictions based on various input data.

The USCIS has long recognized that an economic report provides two data sets of information, "job creation" and "economic impact," both within the geographic scope of the regional center.

Regional Input-Output Modeling Systems (RIMS II)

Effective planning for public- and private-sector projects and programs at the State and local levels requires a systematic analysis of the economic impacts of the projects and programs on affected regions. In turn, systematic analysis of economic impacts must account for the inter-industry relationships within regions because these relationships largely determine how regional economies are likely to respond to project and program changes. Thus, regional input-output (I-O) multipliers, which account for inter industry relationships within regions, are useful tools for regional economic impact analysis.

In the 1970's, the Bureau of Economic Analysis (BEA) developed a method for estimating regional I-O multi-pliers known as RIMS (Regional Industrial Multiplier System), which was based on the work of Garnick and Drake (1) In the 1980's, BEA completed an enhancement of RIMS, known as RIMS II (Regional Input-Output Modeling System), and published a handbook for RIMS II users (2) In 1992, BEA published a second edition of the handbook, in which the multipliers were based on more recent data and improved methodology. Now, BEA is making available a third edition of the handbook, in response to requests by users for additional discussion of the data that they must provide in order to use RIMS II and of the data sources and methods used for multiplier estimation. The multipliers in the third edition reflect I-O data for 1987, the most recent benchmark year for which BEA's national I-O data are available.

RIMS II is based on an accounting framework called an I-O table. For each industry, an I-O table shows the distribution of the inputs purchased and the outputs sold. A typical I-O table in RIMS II is derived mainly from two data sources: BEA's national I-O table, which shows the input and output structure of nearly 500 U.S. industries, and BEA's regional economic accounts, which are used to adjust the national I-O table in order to reflect a region's industrial structure and trading patterns (3).

Using RIMS II for impact analyses has several advantages (4) RIMS II multipliers can be estimated for any region composed of one or more counties and for any industry or group of industries in the national I-O table. The cost of estimating regional multipliers is relatively low because of the accessibility of the main data sources for RIMS II. According to empirical tests, the estimates based on RIMS II are similar in magnitude to the estimates based on relatively expensive surveys (5).

To effectively use the multipliers for impact analysis, users must provide geographically and industrially detailed information on the initial changes in output, earnings, or employment that are associated with the project or program under study. The multipliers can then be used to estimate the total impact of the project or program on regional output, earnings, or employment.

RIMS II is widely used in both the public and private

sector. In the public sector, for example, the Department of Defense uses RIMS II to estimate the regional impacts of military base closings, and State departments of transportation use RIMS II to estimate the regional impacts of airport construction and expansion. In the private sector, analysts, consultants, and economic development practitioners use RIMS II to estimate the regional impacts of a variety of projects, such as the development of theme parks and shopping malls.

1. See Daniel H. Garnick, "Differential Regional Multiplier Models," *Journal of Regional Science* 10 (February 1970): 35–47; and Ronald L. Drake, "A Short-Cut to Estimates of Regional Input-Output Multipliers," *International Regional Science Review* 1 (Fall 1976): 1–17.

2. See U.S. Department of Commerce, Bureau of Economic Analysis, *Regional Input-Output Modeling System (RIMS II): Estimation, Evaluation, and Application of a Disaggregated Regional Impact Model (Washington,* DC: U.S. Government Printing Office, 1981); and U.S. Department of Commerce, Bureau of Economic Analysis, *Regional Multipliers: A User Handbook for the Regional Input-Output Modeling System (RIMS II)(Washington,* DC: U.S. Government Printing Office, 1986).

3. See U.S. Department of Commerce, Bureau of Economic Analysis, *Benchmark Input-Output Accounts of the United States, 1987(Washington,* DC: U.S. Government Printing Office, 1994); and U.S. Department of Commerce, Bureau of Economic Analysis, *Local Area Personal Income, 1969–92* (Washington, DC: U.S. Government Printing Office, 1994).

4. For a discussion of the limitations of using I-O models in impact analysis, see Daniel M. Otto and Thomas G. Johnson, *Microcomputer-Based Input-Output Modeling(Boulder,* CO: Westview Press, 1993), 28–46.

5. See *Regional Input-Output Modeling System (RIMS II),* 39–57; and Sharon M. Brucker, Steven E. Hastings, and William R. Latham III, "The Variation of Estimated Impacts from Five Regional Input-Output Models," *International Regional Science Review* 13 (1990): 119–39.

13
GENERAL ECONOMIC PRINCIPLES, GOOD GROUNDS

The First Law of Economists:
For every economist, there exists an equal and opposite economist.
David Wildasin,

Since 2001 I've been forecasting demand for different types of real estate properties, often finding demand for office and/or warehouse needs, for the purposes of acquisition and development. In 2010 I decided to pursue foreign capital as an alternative way to finance new development deals. As I got deeper into the USCIS EB-5 world, listening to many highly qualified consultants ,including attorneys and economists with impressive resumes, academic degrees and vast experience, I found the very basic principles of economy, employment, supply and demand, etc., started fading from my mind. So I decided to go back to these basics that were effective for our business in the past and that will continue to be so, because they are the general principles of every country's economists.

As a developer, one of my first steps in the due diligence process to acquire land is to order a geotechnical study. Structural and civil engineers use them for many needs in the design process but for me, the real purpose is to understand the strength of the soil, and assure that it will hold the load of the building we are proposing. I deeply believe in the old scripture: *"...He is like a man building a house, who dug down deep and laid the foundation on rock. When a flood came, the torrent struck that house but could not shake it, because it was well built."* (Luke 6:48)

This chapter gives insight into the already established foundations that we have used for our current projects and that have enabled us to successfully obtain approvals from the USCIS since 2012.

My first thought was to start all the way back with Thomas Mun, English writer on economics and author of the book *A Discourse of Trade, from England unto the East Indies* (1621). He believed that a nation's holdings of gold are the main measure of its wealth and that governments should regulate trade to produce an excess of exports over imports in order to gain more gold for the country. This statement is settled in the mind of the people in the U.S. Congress as seen when a Senate Committee Report stated that the EB-5 provision was *"intended to provide new employment for U.S. workers and to infuse new capital in the country*. . . "(underlined by the author) (1). This focus on capital seems easy to understand; providing new employment is where things get tricky.

Type of employments and economic base theory

I was born and raised in a beautiful South American country, Venezuela. There the economy is largely based on the petroleum sector, which since 1976 has been exploited by the government and not open to private corporations. Revenue from petroleum exports accounts for about 18% of the country's GDP and roughly 95% of total exports. Venezuela is the fifth largest member of the **Organization of the Petroleum Exporting Countries (**OPEC) by oil production, so day-to-day, the media is full of comments and news about basic and non-basic industries; the main two divisions of every economy. In primitive times, it was the hunters and gatherers; in contemporary analysis, this division can be thought of as primary versus secondary, productive and nonproductive, export and support, necessary and surplus labor, etc.

Non Basic Employment: These are jobs in activities that produce goods and services produced for consumption in the local community. Examples are jobs in certain service firms, for example, the utilities company, barber shops, etc.

Basic Employment: This refers to jobs in activities that produce more goods and services than can be consumed in the local market, and/or goods produced for consumption outside the community. An example is the automotive industry in Detroit, the plane manufacturing facility of Boeing in Everett, Washington, or the petroleum jobs in Venezuela.

This division of the economy leads to the Economic Base Theory, manifested early in the 1900's by German Sociologist Werner Sombart, who asserts that the way to strengthen and grow the local economy is to develop and enhance the basic sector. The basic sector is therefore identified as the "engine" of the local economy.

"The economic base technique is based on a simple causal model that assumes that the basic sector is the prime cause of local economic

growth, that it is the economic base of the local economy."

(Klosterman, Richard E. 1990. *Community and Analysis Planning Techniques.* Rowmand and Littlefield Publishers, Inc. Savage, Maryland

Economic Base Theory also states that the local economy is strongest when it develops those economic sectors that are not closely tied to the local economy. By producing services or goods that rely primarily on external markets, the local economy can better shield itself from economic downturns because, it is expected, these external markets will remain strong even if the local economy experiences problems. In contrast, a local economy wholly dependent upon local factors will have great trouble responding to economic slumps.

With the Immigration Act of 1990 based on employment creation, Congress sought to bring external capital to the United States by creating a visa program that attracted foreign capital. The program follows the general principle of the Economy Base Theory: create the goods and services that generate income from external sources and are the driving force of the economy.

The same principle was the USCIS Ombudsman's motivation for his memo of March 18th 2009, when he wrote:

> *"In recognition of the present turmoil in the U.S. economy, it is incumbent upon USCIS to take all necessary and appropriate steps to facilitate a healthy, vigorous, and smooth-running employment creation immigrant visa program."*

Following Thomas Mun's statement from the 1600's, the

Ombudsman was looking for an answer to U.S. economic turmoil from the external markets, by converting a visa program into an economic engine fueled by foreign capital.

---

(1)   S. Rep. No. 55, 101st Cong., 1st Sess. at 21 (1989).

14
EMPLOYMENT AND
REAL ESTATE DEMAND

We hear of the wealth of nations, of the powers of production, of the demand and supply of markets, and we forget that these words mean no more, if they mean any thing, then the happiness, and the labor, and the necessities of men.

Francis Wright

Economic Base Theory is used as a method to analyze local-area growth. It examines the extent to which basic employment activities and the inflow of income from exporting goods stimulates growth of the economy, by comparing basic employment to non basic employment. It's an easy method to apply and can predict possible future changes in a region's employment and population.

The Economic Base model recognizes that basic industries create goods and services that can be exported -- activity that in turn creates employment for industries that generate services and goods for the local economy's own consumption (non-basic). By adding both types of employment, it is possible to define the *total* employment of the area. This total employment picture of a specific area defines the need for office space and/or industrial space and will also impact growth in the area population (more employees, more households). This new population drives demand for housing, as well as a variety of services and goods, leading providers of these local services to demand space for more retail and office space and more employees. This process is explained in the following chart:

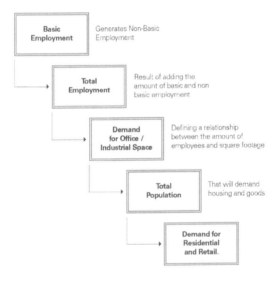

This cause-consequence relationship is the general principle that the USCIS economists have referred to in many responses to applications based on tenant occupancy when they stated:

"...the demand for labor precedes the decision

about where to house that labor as a general economic principle…"

In the next chapter we'll take a closer look at the applicant's economic assumptions about job creation and the USCIS position based on the general economic principle.

15
JOB CREATION BASED ON
TENANT OCCUPANCY

*We are too much accustomed to attribute to a single cause that which
is the product of several, and the majority of our controversies
come from that.*

Marcus Aurelius

To comply with EB-5 program requirements on Job Creation, economists supporting the business case for USCIS approval began using what they felt were reasonable methodologies. They projected the number of jobs that would result from developing real estate space.

Arguments to support such job creation are contained in the following section from an econometric study of a real world case:

> "...For this project, XX examined the economic effects of professional center operations on the region. XX systematically reviewed each set of assumptions used to properly customize the over

440 sector outputs that make up the econometric model's set matrixes. XX applied specific sector data resulting in a very detailed, realistic and logical range of likely outcomes. XX/IMPLAN-modeled simulations were based on the following assumptions:

• *The investment in the real estate property would create XXXX jobs for the purposes of EB-5.*

• *Operational employment demand will remain constant throughout the simulation horizon.*

The definition of "direct jobs" used in this report should not be confused with the concept of direct job creation measurable by Forms I-9, payroll records or other similar documentation as set forth in 8 C.F.R. § 204.6(i)(4)(i)(A). That section contemplates jobs created by the actual employees of the new commercial enterprise, specifically in the non-regional center context.

When economists use the term "direct" jobs in the context of an econometric methodology such as IMPLAN, what is meant are jobs created directly by revenues (which in the EB-5 Pilot program results from an immigrant investor's investment). For example, where a regional center-based new commercial enterprise comprised of immigrant investors renovates a building it purchases, the employees of the various unaffiliated tenants of that building would be considered "direct" jobs in the context of an econometric report. However, those jobs are not

"direct" in the sense set forth in 8 C.F.R. §
204.6(i) (4) (i) (A) where the new commercial
enterprise is itself the employer that can provide
Form I-9 or other similar documentation on its
own employees. The tenants' employees are not
"direct" employees of the regional center-based
new commercial enterprise.

In keeping with the EB-5 guidelines, the number
of construction jobs for all types of buildings is
based on "hard costs" of construction activity and
does not include "soft costs" architectural and
engineering fees, permits and construction fees,
contingency allowances, sales commissions,
financing, legal, insurance costs associated with
the construction activity, overhead and profits.
Also, purchases of furniture, fixtures, equipment,
telecommunications and computers are not
included in any of the calculations, because these
purchases will generally be made from
manufacturers and suppliers outside the area. In
this analysis, the land on which these buildings
will be constructed has previously been purchased
and is not part of the cost estimates…"

The assumption that investing in new office space would create jobs is clearly contrary to Economic Base Theory's cause-and-effect relationship of employment and real estate space, as explained in the previous chapter. You'll recall that under Economic Base Theory, basic employment industries create jobs in the non-basic employment industries, and lead to growth in total employment of a community, which *only then* generates the need for additional real estate space.

Developers' assumptions supporting EB-5 development projects did not conform to sound economic theory, as the following chart shows. Note that the "build it and jobs will come" approach, as shown by the arrows, <u>reverses the widely accepted job creation flow of Economic Base Theory.</u>

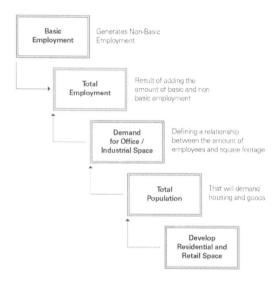

These assumptions have been rejected by the USCIS since February 2012, with many statements such as:

> *"...USCIS has concerns that the attribution of these direct jobs to the EB-5 investment may not be based on reasonable economic methodologies, and therefore do not demonstrate in 'verifiable detail' that the requisite jobs will be created."*

In the USCIS' view, job creation comes to a specific area from the basic and non-basic employment activities performed by the tenants who will occupy the future building, and it seems" to have no cause-effect relationship with the foreign capital invested for construction of the building that will house such activities.

These are reasonable generic economist principles, but how can we overcome this challenge and continue to use foreign capital?

The solution was provided by a USCIS economist in the agency's Request for Evidence issued in 2012.

16
UNEMPLOYMENT AND VACANCY
RATES RATIOS

*Governments will always play a huge part in solving big problems.
They set public policy and are uniquely able to provide the resources to
make sure solutions reach everyone who needs them. They also fund
basic research, which is a crucial component of the innovation
that improves life for everyone.*

Bill Gates

As mentioned before, I was raised in South America,
where the majority of the governments in many countries
are authoritarian. Citizens don't have much say;
governmental agencies impose criteria and decisions with
no room for public opinion or opportunity for the citizens
to exercise any of their rights, not even the constitutional
ones. So it is amazing to me to watch the democracy of
the great country of the United States of America every
day and to see how a federal Agency like the USCIS
proposes a solution to the problem that the applicant

himself created, in order to provide an opportunity to enjoy the benefits the immigration law intends to grant.

This process is an expression of a government agency that understands it is part of a society where the individual citizens hold the power, and the right, to influence decisions made about how their country will be governed and have the right to say and write what they wish.

Let's look at the USCIS' early solution to the job creation challenge: establishing that there is a cause/effect relationship between the construction of new real estate space and the tenants who will perform the economic activities that generate jobs. In order to establish that this Tenant Occupancy job generation methodology is reasonable and appropriate, the USCIS proposed that if a local economy's total employment growth is constrained due to lack of real estate space for employees to perform their economic activities, the construction of a building to house such labor will be recognized as a job creation activity.

There are two steps -- aligned with the Economic Base model flow -- to document this is the case with your project. You'll need to credibly document that there is excess demand for the space you will create, and explain how you'll verify that the tenants occupying your space will create new jobs, rather than relocating existing jobs. Look to the USCIS requirements below:

> *Provide evidence that there is excess demand for the specific types of tenants (various tenants as indicated in the business plan and economic analysis for your construction project and business plan.) Please provide a data-based assessment, and the source of data utilized by the assessment.*
>
> *To show such excess demand, the assessment*

should:

Analyze: whether prospective tenants which would locate in the commercial space that will be constructed and/or renovated under the proposed project are currently suffering from a lack of a unique or specialized business space, that, in economic terms, such prospective tenants are "constrained" from commencing or expanding their businesses by a lack of unique or specialized business space.

Provide a data-based analysis, including the source of data, which establishes whether there is "pent-up" demand for the specific professional and business services relevant to your project. Such data-based analysis should include:

Evidence of congestion externalities as demonstrated by a low vacancy-unemployment ratio pursuant to specific space and businesses seeking to expand, respectively; and

Evidence of upward wage and rental pressures in specific regional sectors that are likely to be attracted to the proposed project space.

The jobs that become located within the tenant space of the project should be shown to be a result of an expansion in specific services driven by your project as opposed to tenant shifting and/or relocation of already-existing jobs. Please explain how it will be verified that the jobs that will become located within the tenant space of the project can be considered "new" jobs.

In 2009 the USCIS issued the Neufeld memo, which asked

for the creation of a set of rules and regulations for processing EB5 visas – a step the administration had failed to take. It turned out that the current regulation is an informal gathering of several memos published since then with many responses to applications as Request for Evidence (RFE). By December 2012, the policy for job creation based on tenant occupancy was defined with several criteria.

The USCIS details three issues of concern on this matter:

1) **Evidence that tenants are likely to occupy the commercial space**: That is, there is concern that once a shopping mall or office building is finished, the space will be largely vacant. To allay this concern, the developer must provide::

   a. A description of the products and services to be provided. *Footnote this instead? Matter of Ho, 22 I&N Dec. 206, 213 (Assoc. Cmm'r 1998),*

   b. Marketing plan as discussed is to be part of the comprehensive business plan, which provides support of new tenant occupancy in the region.

   c. Detailed Market analysis,

      i. Including the names of competing businesses

      ii. their relative strengths and weaknesses,

      iii. A comparison of the competition's products and pricing structures,

      iv. A description of the target market/prospective customers of the new commercial enterprise. *Matter of Ho, 22 I&N Dec. 206, 213 (Assoc. Cmm'r 1998)*

      v. The current size of the market;

vi. Historic trends and developing trends;

vii. Projected growth rate;

viii. The target market and number and purchase of potential customers;

ix. Distinguishing characteristics of the target market and why potential tenants are likely to come to this new building/mall; existing competitors in the market and distinguishing features in relation to existing competitors.

x. The market analysis may include data collected on trends and size and purchases in the target market.

xi. Market test results from potential tenants who were contacted and interviewed.

d. Evidence on lack of appropriate space in the geographical region where the applicant is constructing its commercial space. The following are examples of evidence of lack of appropriate space:

e. Evidence of low vacancy rates of commercial space within the geographical region where the project is located.

f. Evidence that, even if vacancy rates of general commercial space are high, there is a lack of suitable commercial space, such as space with the amenities and specialized facilities required for the tenants that are expected to lease from the commercial enterprise. Supporting materials showing available and suitable commercial space in the region and the characteristics of the commercial space which makes it unfit to satisfy the ability to set up the types of businesses and outlets indicated in the business plan.

g. The applicant can provide responses from surveys of employers (a minimal sample size of 50 is recommended) in the geographic region indicating that lack of appropriate space is a main constraint towards setting up a business in this geographic region.

h. A detailed letter from a state or local governmental official, such as the Mayor of the city where the development will occur or an official of an economic development agency in the area, describing and providing supporting evidence of the availability of suitable space or lack thereof. For example, supporting evidence may include a study conducted on behalf of the city addressing constraints on business development in the area.

i. Evidence that the new commercial space will bring substantial cost savings to the tenants who lease space there. The following types of evidence can be useful in this regard:

j. Evidence of lower operational and/or maintenance costs to the lessee in the commercial space.

k. Tax benefits, rebates, or other subsidies to the lessee.

l. Evidence that demand for commercial space is growing in the geographical area where the RC is constructing commercial space.

m. Evidence of growing demand for leasing space includes:

n. Evidence that lease prices for commercial spaces are increasing.

o. Evidence of increased demand in the area through population growth, income growth and consumption growth in the area.

p. Evidence that new tenants and customers will be attracted to the commercial space due to the construction of the project. This may be particularly relevant in the case of Targeted Employment Areas, whether they are high unemployment areas or rural areas. Examples of evidence that can be useful to show that the EB-5 project is more likely than not to attract new tenants and customers includes:

q. Evidence that an anchor tenant (e.g. a tenant that will occupy one of the largest available spaces within the development) has already been attracted or is likely to sign a lease for this commercial space. In this case, the applicant can provide verifiable evidence in the form of the actual lease or a previous relation and previous leases with the anchor tenant in similar projects from the commercial enterprise.

r. Evidence of new businesses coming into the geographical area for the first time and locating in the commercial development, offering products or services that were not otherwise available in that market, as well as agreements or letters of intent from actual or potential new businesses.

s. Support letter from the local government showing preferred status for this economic development area, indicating that funds are being invested in the area in the form of roads, bridges or other infrastructure.

2) **Confirmation that the tenant jobs will be "new" jobs and not "merely relocated":** The jobs that become located within the tenant space of the project should be shown to be more likely than not a result of an expansion in specific services driven by the project as opposed to merely tenant shifting and/or re-location of already existing jobs.

a. Please explain how it will be verified that the jobs that will become located within the tenant space of the project can be considered "new" jobs.

b. Second, the counting of tenant jobs relies on the assumption that these jobs are not simply jobs relocated from commercial space somewhere else, e.g. relocated from another commercial space within the same geographical area.

c. Lastly, information on "the marketing strategy of the business," as discussed in *Matter of Ho,* should also be included to support new tenant occupancy in the Regional Center.

3) Evidence that the job creation estimates are reasonable: If the applicant can show that it is more likely than not the local area's economic conditions and specific benefits provided by the proposed commercial space that will cause new tenant businesses to start operations in the commercial space, the applicant must also present a credible methodology that estimates industry-specific tenant employment levels. The applicant should prepare employment estimates using detailed, verifiable, and transparent methodologies with supporting data. USCIS encourages you to provide information regarding the specific industry of projected tenants as well as the projected revenue/square footage metrics that are used in the input-output model to support the number of projected tenant jobs.

17
BUSINESS PLAN:
MATTER OF HO

It takes as much energy to wish as it does to plan.
Eleanor Roosevelt

In 1998, the USCIS Associate Commissioner made a determination in the matter of *In re Ho* (commonly referred to as MATTER OF HO). This determination was and continues to be significant to the preparation of mandated EB-5 Business Plans, since it explicitly details that the EB-5 related regulations require "a **comprehensive** Business Plan."

Business Plans submitted with EB-5 visa petitions must provide a basis for the reviewing agency to draw "reasonable inferences" about the business' potential viability. The more detailed the business plan, the better the opportunity for the reviewing agency to determine the proposed business' potential for success.

The USCIS decision to deny the immigration petition in Matter of Ho detailed the criteria for a business plan.

The following is an easy to understand checklist of what should be included in a business plan, based on the Matter of Ho decision, with some added examples:

The plan should include a description of the business, laid out in an organized and logical manner. The USCIS must be able to follow the timeline for a clear picture of the business. Provide basic facts about the company, mission statement and goals to give the USCIS examiner a good place to start the determination as to whether the visa seeker is proposing a viable and reasonable business that will meet all EB-5 requirements.

Also include in the business plan: the organization's business objectives; a market analysis including names of competing real estate developments and their relative strengths and weaknesses; a comparison of the competition's products and pricing structures; a description of the target market and prospective customers; a description of any manufacturing or production processes, materials required and supply sources; details of any contracts executed; marketing strategy including pricing, advertising, and servicing; organizational structure; and sales, cost and income projections and details of the bases therefore. In addition, specifically with respect to employment, the business plan must set forth the development company's personnel experience, staffing requirements and, job descriptions for all positions related to the project., and a timetable with rationale for hiring within the next two years.

18
INVESTMENT AT RISK
MATTER OF IZUMMI

Risk is supposed to be about choice and consequence;
you take a chance and you win or you lose.
Rodrigo Azpúrua.

Risk-taking is not just about a single big leap. It requires not just momentary bravery, but sustained courage to endure uncertainty and the lonely experience of living off an idea that may not succeed. "Creativity and discovery necessarily involve risk, so there will be dark days for you," said Alan Heeger after winning the Nobel Prize in physics, "but dealing with that risk is a part of the thrill and satisfaction."

The EB-5 Program is seeking to attract individuals from other countries who are willing to put their capital at risk in the United States, with the hope of a return on their investment, to help create U.S. jobs. The law does not specify what the degree of risk must be; the entire amount of capital need only be at risk to some degree

A well accepted definition for **risk** is the potential of loss (an undesirable outcome, however, not necessarily so) resulting from a given action, activity and/or inaction. The notion implies that a choice having an influence on the outcome sometimes exists (or existed). Potential losses themselves may also be called "risks."

Any human endeavor carries some risk, but some are much riskier than others.

Risk can be defined in seven different ways:

1. The probability of something happening multiplied by the resulting cost or benefit if it does.

2. The probability or threat of quantifiable damage, injury, liability, loss, or any other negative occurrence that is caused by external or internal vulnerabilities, and that may be avoided through preemptive action.

3. In respect to finance, risk is: the probability that an actual return on an investment will be lower than the expected return. Financial risk can be divided into the following categories: basic risk, capital risk, country risk, default risk, delivery risk, economic risk, exchange rate risk, interest rate risk, liquidity risk, operations risk, payment system risk, political risk, refinancing risk, reinvestment risk, settlement risk, sovereign risk and underwriting risk.

There is a common misconception regarding what comprises an investment. In many countries where there is a high inflation rate and the present value of money is high, people purchase an asset and consider it as an investment because the liquid money that loses value over time is exchanged for an asset that gains value over time.

If the immigrant investor is guaranteed the return of a portion of his or her investment, or is guaranteed a rate of return on a portion of his or her investment, then that portion of the capital is not at risk.

In a decision from USCIS named *Matter of Izummi*, 22 I&N Dec. at 180-188, the risk was defined as:

> *For the capital to be "at risk" there must be a risk of loss and a chance for gain. In our precedent decision Matter of Izummi, 22 I&N Dec. at 183-188, the AAO found that the capital was not at risk because the investment was governed by a redemption agreement that protected against the risk of loss of the capital and, therefore, constituted an impermissible debt arrangement under 8 C.F.R. § 204.6(e) as it was no different from the risk any business creditor incurs. Id. at 185. Furthermore, a promise to return any portion of the immigrant investor's minimum required capital negates the required element of risk. Thus, if the agreement between the new commercial enterprise and immigrant investor, such as a limited partnership agreement or operating agreement, provides that the investor may demand return of or redeem some portion of capital after obtaining conditional lawful permanent resident status (i.e., following approval of the investor's Form I-526 and subsequent visa issuance or, in the case of adjustment, approval of the investor's Form I-485), that portion of capital is not at risk. Similarly, if the investor is individually guaranteed the right to eventual ownership or use of a particular asset in consideration of the investor's contribution of capital into the new commercial enterprise, such as a home (or other real estate interest) or item of personal property, the expected present value of the guaranteed ownership or use of such asset does not count toward the total amount of the investor's capital contribution in determining how much money was truly placed at risk.*

Cf. Izummi at 184 concludes that an investment cannot be considered a qualifying contribution of capital at risk to the extent of a guaranteed return. Nothing, however, precludes an investor from receiving a return on his or her capital (i.e., a distribution of profits) during or after the conditional residency period, so long as prior to or during the two-year conditional residency period, and before the requisite jobs have been created, the return is not a portion of the investor's principal investment and was not guaranteed to the investor.

An investor's money may be held in escrow until the investor has obtained conditional lawful permanent resident status if the immediate and irrevocable release of the escrowed funds is contingent only upon approval of the investor's Form I-526 and subsequent visa issuance and admission to the United States as a conditional permanent resident or, in the case of adjustment of status, approval of the investor's Form I-485.

An investor's funds may be held in escrow within the United States to avoid any evidentiary issues that may arise with respect to issues such as significant currency fluctuations and foreign capital export restrictions. Use of foreign escrow accounts, however, is not prohibited as long as the petition establishes that it is more likely than not that the minimum qualifying capital investment will be transferred to the new commercial enterprise in the United States upon the investor obtaining conditional lawful permanent resident status. At the Form I-829 stage, USCIS will require evidence verifying that the escrowed funds were released and that the investment was sustained in the new commercial enterprise.

It is important to minimize the risk in the business plan and the corporate documents so that we as developers reduce that amount of risk, but still comply with the requirement of the Matter of Izummi.

Alexis de Tocqueville wrote, "Those living in the instability of a democracy have the constant image of chance before them, and in the end, they come to like all those projects in which chance plays a part ... not only because of the promise of profit but because they like the emotions evoked."

Conclusion

Risk-taking as nourishment for the soul is a fundamental American principle and has been with us since the nation's earliest days.

19
RISK AND
CORPORATE LAW

It may be true that the law cannot make a man love me, but it can keep him from lynching me, and I think that's pretty important.

Martin Luther King, Jr.

This is another convergent point in the EB-5 Visas business, where the complicated rules of the Securities Exchange Commission (SEC), which regulate all offerings of any stock, share or securities of any type, (private or public), merge with the USCIS regulations regarding types of risk.

At the beginning of every project, all the tasks facing the development are uncertain. The risk is higher, because no one knows if those tasks will be completed and the business objectives achieved. To mitigate risk, U.S. laws are very protective of the consumer and the public.

The main spirit of the SEC law is to identify and explain the risks of an investment in one document, the Private Placement Memorandum, with a caveat to all prospective investors to carefully read all its documents and exhibits. The language of the SEC's document is fairly standard.

With an EB-5 real estate development investment as its context, the following sample private placement memorandum paraphrases the most important disclosures that the law requires. It provides a sense of how such a risk is treated under U.S. laws:

SAMPLE PRIVATE PLACEMENT LANGUAGE:

Such a memorandum does not purport to be all-inclusive or contain all the information that a prospective investor may require in investigating the partnership or evaluating an investment.

In making an investment decision, prospective investors must rely on their own examination of the partnership and the terms of the offering, including, without limitation, the merits and risks involved.

Risk is inherent in the nature of the Real Estate Development Business, The time and costs required to complete the Project may be substantially increased by many factors, including shortages of materials, equipment, technical skills and labor, adverse weather conditions, natural disasters, labor disputes, disputes with contractors, accidents, changes in government priorities and policies, delays in obtaining the requisite licenses, permits and approvals from the relevant authorities, and other unforeseeable problems and circumstances. These problems may delay construction and increase costs, which in turn would delay completion of the Project and the developer's ability to generate cash flow, and which can significantly reduce projected rates of return and the developer's ability to service debt costs, including repayment of the Loan.

Obtaining building permits is a time-consuming process, and it is virtually impossible to ordinarily predict how long it may take to receive final building permits, however all of the necessary building permits are currently ready for issuance when requested by the developer and the payment of necessary fees.

Usually this uncertainty could result in construction delays and increased costs associated with the Project. The costs of construction materials and labor may change to the detriment of the Developer during the course of construction.

Unanticipated cost increases may require the Developer to raise or borrow additional capital, which may or may not be available, to complete construction of the Project.

Many of those risks are analyzed and discovered at the due diligence stage, while others become evident later, in forward-looking statements or in the operation of the business.

Among the most important risks of Real Estate Development are:

Zoning Approvals. The required zoning approvals have been obtained in order to develop the Project in accordance with the current business plan. There are no assurances that the business plan may not have to be modified accordingly, or that additional or modified zoning approvals will not be needed. However, the

Developer believes that the approvals currently obtained will be sufficient.

Timing of Completion. A time schedule for the completion of improvements and substantial stabilization of the Project is included in the Business Plan. There are no assurances that such time schedule can be satisfied, and if the timing for the completion of development is delayed by any significant degree, then the cost of said development will increase accordingly.

Cost Overruns. Cost overruns may be encountered as a result of numerous factors, including not only the delay in the development process, the failure of certain contracted parties to complete their work in accordance with the contracted amount, necessitating the substitution of subcontractors and potential increases in pricing. Furthermore, unforeseen issues may be encountered that otherwise require an increase in the development budget that has not otherwise been reserved for in the contingency fund.

Marketing and Operating Efforts May Not Be Successful. The Project represents a commercial development project and will include certain commercial lease agreements with varying rates and terms. There are no assurances that the Developer will be able to successfully manage the various business elements of the Project and market its concept in a manner that achieves the projected rates, volume and profit as set forth in the financial projections contained in the Project Business Plan. In particular, each component of the Project, namely the office construction and leasing and operation, has its own unique operating and marketing attributes and will be dependent upon numerous factors, including consumer and commercial demand for the products to be delivered in the specific area that comprise

EB-5 Visas & Real Estate Development

the Project. There are no assurances that marketing and operating efforts will be successful.

The Investment in the Project is Speculative. Investing in real estate as contemplated by the Developer involves an inherent exposure to fluctuations in the real estate market, including the availability of financing, increases in mortgage rates and borrowing rates and general economic conditions, and there is no assurance that its investment strategy will be successful. Prospective Investors should not subscribe for Units unless they can afford a loss of all their capital invested in the Company as a result of the non-payment of the Loan.

The Company's Investment is Illiquid. The Project may not be easy to liquidate or refinance. No assurance can be given that the investment will be paid or when it will be paid.

The Project Will be Subject to Typical Real Estate Investment Risks. The typical risks relating to an investment in real estate will apply to an investment in the Project including, but not limited to, the national, regional and local economic climates, competitive market forces, changes in market values, changes in market rates of interest and competition from other existing competing properties and new competing properties that may be developed in the future.

The Project may be subject to technical risks and technology risks. The Project may be subject to technical risks, including design errors, defects in construction and materials, mechanical breakdown, failure to perform according to design specifications and other unanticipated events, which adversely affect operations, health, safety and other equipment and/or plant facilities. While the Project will be insured and it is expected that third parties will bear much of this risk, there can be no assurance that any or all such risk can be mitigated or that such parties, if present, will perform their obligations.

Service. Interest rates for the financing of real estate are at historically low levels, and any increase in rates may have an adverse effect on the Developer's ability to pay debt service associated with any loans, including the Loan. In addition, increases in interest rates may have an adverse effect on the operation and/or sale of the Project and may have an adverse effect on the ability of the Developer to refinance the Project and, thus, its ability to pay the Loan.

Risks Relating to Businesses Contained in Project. The businesses contained in the Project will be subject to various environmental, health and safety laws, regulations and permit requirements. The Project is subject to changing and increasingly stringent environmental, health and safety laws, regulations and permit requirements, and there can be no guarantee that all costs and risks regarding compliance with environmental laws and regulations can be identified. New and more stringent environmental, health and safety laws, regulations and permit requirements or stricter interpretations of current laws or regulations could impose substantial additional costs on the Project and the business operated thereunder.

Summarizing, the ultimate intention of the SEC law is to warn the public that when they intend to invest, they should not do so unless they can afford a loss of all their capital invested in the Company. The law intends to show and disclose the risks involved, assuring that the investor is aware of all the work and uncertainty of outcomes. involved.

The SEC's conclusion:
INVESTORS ARE ON THEIR OWN.

Developers should expect the closest scrutiny from investors, and their attonreys at all stages of EB-5 project development. Following sound fundraising practices and adhering strictly to the legal framework involved must be the first priority of anyone engaged in EB-5 visas fundraising.

20

HOW TO SETUP A SUCCESSFUL
EB-5 PROJECT

"Screw it, Let's do it!"
Richard Branson

Measuring performance is essential to drive the success of every EB-5 development project. Businesses worldwide rely on performance indicators, or key performance indicators (KPIs), which are measurement tools that can assess overall performance or evaluate specific projects. I consider KPIs to be the cornerstone of the planning process, and they should be set immediately after the vision.

In our organization, Riviera Point Development Group, we define success in terms of making progress toward strategic goals. That demands knowing what is most important to the organization from the outset. 'What is important' often depends on the stakeholders who have interest in the project. On a real estate project funded by EB-5 investors, for example, the KPIs are completely different than those for a project funded with a construction loan from a community bank.

Choosing the right KPIs takes discipline and intensive strategy. A common way to choose KPIs is to apply a management framework such as the "balanced scorecard." Both the KPI and balanced scorecard concepts were introduced in the late 1990's by Dr. Robert S. Kaplan, the Marvin Bower Professor of Leadership Development at Harvard Business School and former dean of Carnegie-Mellon University. Dr. Kaplan also received a Ph.D. in Operations Research from Cornell University.

The KPI and the balanced scorecard concepts, as put forth by Dr. Kaplan and co-author David P. Norton, are now recognized globally as a critical foundation in a holistic strategy-execution process that helps organizations articulate and execute actionable strategy.

In setting our organization's KPIs, we follow "SMART" criteria. This ensures each indicator has a **specific** business purpose and is **measurable** to really get the value of the KPI. The defined norms have to be **achievable**, and the improvement in a KPI has to be **relevant** to the success of the organization. Finally, it must be **time-phased,** meaning the value or outcomes are shown for a predefined and relevant period.

For an EB-5 development project, KPIs must addresses one of the most basic aspects of "what is important" -- minimizing investors' exposure to the risks inherent in the real estate development business.

Wealthy foreign nationals looking to invest $500,000 or $1,000,000 are typically very smart entrepreneurs with a clear understanding of business and the risks involved.

To assess how your project minimizes risks, they'll want to know:

Specifics: Does your project comply with the EB-5 Program's legal framework? Is the Regional Center approved? Does the project already have any applicant with a I-526 application approved?

Measurable: The project's cost and job-creation capacity must be accurately measured in advance.

Attainable: How will you achieve your goal? Do you have a well established plan; what tools are you using, and what are your strengths in equity, management, etc.

Relevant: Is the project's size appropriate for the number of investors you seek – and for meeting the market's need? Does the development team have the capacity to raise the funds to complete the project, and do they have the knowledge and experience to complete what they plan to start?

Time Bound: Can your project accomplish the job-creation requirement within the time frame set by the immigration laws?

Developers need to demonstrate that they are proactively minimizing all risks. For example, it's common for an EB-5 investor's money to go into an escrow account as a first step, not into the project. Those funds often remain in escrow until an investor's application for visa is granted by the USCIS. That helps limit the investor's risk to the amount of the legal fees, rather than the total capital contribution. There are many other ways to reduce investors' risk. Each time you find a risk in your project, find a way to reduce its impact, and you'll have a product that will be attractive to the public worldwide.

(1) Kaplan, Robert S., and D. P. Norton. *The Strategy-Focused Organization: How Balanced Scorecard Companies Thrive in the New Business Environment.* Boston, MA: Harvard Business School Press, 2000.

ABOUT THE AUTHOR

Rodrigo Azpúrua is a regular speaker and consultant on how to invest in solid and approved EB-5 projects. He has spoken for a wide range of audiences in locations as diverse as Miami, Orlando, Caracas, Buenos Aires, Quito, Shanghai, Shenzhen and Hong Kong, and has appeared on CNN, Fox News, in Florida Trend magazine and the Miami Herald and
Sun-Sentinel, among other media.

He has a Law Degree from Universidad Santa María in Caracas, Venezuela, and for 14 years he practiced real estate law and international law. He is a member of the globally-recognized Project Management Institute (PMI) and has been directly responsible for the management of over $200,000,000 of Land Development projects that created a total of more than 1 million square feet of office space in seven
different locations in the State of Florida.

He is also a Certified Commercial Investment Member (CCIM). The CCIM designation is often referred to as the PhD of Commercial Real Estate.

Rodrigo Azpúrua started and integrated the Riviera Point Development Group as a professional team of financial, real estate management and development specialists committed to the use of private and foreign equity to develop quality buildings, enhance Florida's communities and generate jobs for America, with a business formula that accounts for all stages of the economic cycle. In addition to developing EB-5 funded commercial real estate projects throughout South Florida, Rodrigo joint ventures with other developers who seek foreign investment to finance projects.